PIANO FREEDOM

HOW TO TRANSFORM YOUR PIANO PLAYING FOREVER FOR THE BETTER

TERESA WONG

Copyright © 2016 Wong Wing Yin
All rights reserved.
ISBN: 978-988-77083-0-8

All rights reserved. No part of this book may be reproduced or transmitted in any form or by any means, electronic or mechanical, including photocopying, recording, or any information storage and retrieval system without prior written permission of the Author. Your support of Author's rights is appreciated.

To my Grandma May.

TABLE OF CONTENTS

PREFACE: Piano Technique is a Myth 1
CHAPTER ONE: The Importance of a Positive Attitude 3
CHAPTER TWO: Body Orientation and Exercises.......................... 5
    Lower Body... 7
    Body Awareness Exercise: Lower and Upper Body 12
    Shoulders 14
    Upper Arms 15
    Forearms.. 16
CHAPTER THREE: Finger-Forearm Alignment 19
    Hands 22
    Palms... 23
    Wrists 24
    Fingers... 27
CHAPTER FOUR: The "Think Big" Exercise................................... 33
CHAPTER FIVE: Bernstein's Weight Training Method 37
CHAPTER SIX: Sándor's Five Basic Motions 47
    Five-fingers, Scales and Arpeggios 50
    Rotation 56
    Staccato 58
    Free Fall 60
    Thrust 63
CHAPTER SEVEN: My Methodology.. 67
CHAPTER EIGHT: Practice Makes Perfect: Only If You Know How ... 71

CHAPTER TEN: Why Do You Want To Learn Piano?.................... 93
VIDEOS.. 99
AFTERWORD 101
RECOMMENDED BOOKLIST 103
ABOUT THE AUTHOR.. 109

PREFACE
PIANO TECHNIQUE IS A MYTH

When I was young, I did not understand or believe in 'piano technique'. I thought, probably as I was being taught and influenced by various teachers, that I just needed to practice more, and good technique would come naturally.

Yet gradually, I found that even with hours of practice, my playing did not improve as much as I wanted to. I started to wonder if there was a problem with my practicing. One should be able to play much better after a lot of practice, right? At first, I did not know how to advance my technique, so naturally I asked my teachers, but none gave me the answer I needed. Some simply told me to practice more, while others made it sound like technique was some kind of myth or God-gifted talent that could not be attained by just trying or working hard. Nonetheless, I did not believe that answer. I desperately wanted to strengthen my technique, so I would not feel tired playing a difficult repertoire even after hours of practice. More importantly, I wanted to be able to control my playing and express myself in the way I wanted. Therefore, I set off on my own personal journey to find the truth about piano technique.

I was a bookworm who loved to submerge myself in books, so I went to libraries to search for what I needed. I learned there were countless books on this topic. I cannot say that I read all of them page by page, but I did take the time for a quick read of whatever I got and found that most of them were both boring and unhelpful.

With determination and persistence, I discovered two books: Seymour Bernstein's *With Your Own Two Hands* and György Sándor's *On Piano Playing*. These are the two books that helped me the most in improving my technique — indeed, they forever transformed my playing and my understanding about this subject. I am not saying I now have the best technique in the world by any stretch, but I do want to share with all of you, my students and readers, what I have learned, as I believe that knowledge will help you as well. Having solid technique gives you much more ease in your playing and greater personal musical expression. It grants you freedom, and the feeling of being free at the piano is tremendous. It is a feeling of complete confidence and emotional harmony. Reading this book is important, but so is trying out the technique and exercises offered in it. Have fun with the methods here! You will find that improving your technique is more than just drilling Hanon and Czerny exercises mindlessly.

Who says you cannot enjoy your playing while being serious about it at the same time?

You can! Let's get started!

Teresa Wong

CHAPTER ONE
THE IMPORTANCE OF HAVING A POSITIVE ATTITUDE

When you first read this title, you probably may have thought, 'What does attitude have to do with piano playing?' First, you have to understand that your mind always comes first, before your body. Your mind controls your body ('No, my body is out of control! I cannot control my fingers!'). You think before you act. Yes, you do, and if you don't, you wouldn't even be reading this book! Patience and Control are the two words you should hold on to steadfastly.

Now let's talk about having the right mindset for your piano playing. If you want to improve, you have to believe you can improve, instead of just thinking, 'I can never get better even if I try!' So from here on, think and believe that 'I can play better'! Okay, once you believe that you can, next you have to believe that I can do what you need. Yes, you have to believe that I can help you and that my method works before you go ahead and read and try it. If you think my method is not good ('Why should I listen to you?), then I can assure you that it will not work for you at all. Today, it is difficult for us to trust ourselves and also trust others. However, start from here, and start from now with a positive mindset. This new attitude will bring you closer to your freedom at the piano every single day.

CHAPTER TWO

LESSON ONE: BODY ORIENTATION AND EXERCISES

Having the right sitting posture from the start facilitates the most efficient use of the body during piano playing. Follow the simple steps below:

- Sit at the piano.
- Stay focused and pay attention.
- Sit up straight and do not crouch.
- To sit up, straighten yourself up all the way upwards from your lower back. Immediately you can feel your whole back being pulled up from the bottom of your spine.
- Do not lean back. Instead, try leaning forward just a little.

When you do lean forward, do not round your back. Open your shoulders and chest and move your chest forward. Tilt your pelvic bones back, so that you can fold your upper body forward at your hip crease. This movement will allow you to feel more of your whole body weight channeling all the way down under your round fingertips and deep into the keys. It is also important to plant your feet firmly on the ground. Both feet should be flat right from the beginning before you begin to play, and they should bear the same weight underneath so as to provide balance and support and let your arms and hands remain light and easily movable at all times.

Note that when you do become more comfortable and experienced in incorporating your body weight into your playing, you will start transferring your weight, shifting your body and moving it around, and your feet would then move from their starting position to various spots on the ground accordingly.

Figure 1. Correct Posture

LOWER BODY

The lower body position is also very important because it helps you transfer your body weight into your playing. Keep the following points in mind:

- Adjust the height of the piano bench to a level where your thighs are more or less parallel to the floor (unless you are a shorter or taller build, then you might need to sit a little higher or lower), and you are not sitting either too high or too low, but just right.
- You should feel your body weight under your feet solidly, and sense that your feet are grounded to the floor.
- Your forearms should also be more or less parallel to the floor.

Figure 2. Young girl at the piano

> Note: For those young children whose feet are not touching the ground yet when sitting on the piano bench, place a small stool or a stable block for them on which can firmly plant their feet.

Remember that from now on, you do not just play with your fingers. You want to use the energy of your whole body. That is why you have to sit properly at the piano with both feet firmly grounded on the floor, your seat bones securely situated on the piano bench, so you can move your upper body to the either side, as well as to the front and back whenever necessary. Remember that the distance between your two feet should be significantly wider than the seat bone, to the degree that you feel your body weight firmly secured to the ground but without losing your balance when you move toward the four planes (left, right, front and back). No crossing legs, crouching backs, shrugging shoulders, or tightening of the upper arms. Sit like you mean to play well is the ideal first step to playing right. *

> *Note: After you know how to maneuver your body weight effortlessly in the autopilot mode (i.e. without having to think about how to move your body when you play), you can sit however you feel like – you might have noticed the various ways that famous pianists sit in front of the piano, higher or lower at the bench, crouching over the instrument with the back super-curled, leaning backward and swaying the body vigorously, or sitting quietly with almost no body movement at all. Still, at the beginning when you try to incorporate your body weight and acquire weight transfer skill, it is best for you to sit up straight with both feet flat on the ground as I suggest above.*

If you are not sure you are sitting properly, try standing from your sitting position at the piano with your feet firmly grounded on the floor without any help from your hands (no supporting yourself to stand up with hands pushing against the bench or the piano). If you can do that, then your sitting position is correct.

> *Watch Technique Transformation Course Video 1: Sitting Posture and Body Weight Shift*

Another method is to place a full body mirror next to the piano to observe your own sitting position. It is a good way to see the way you sit while you play. If a mirror is not available, ask a friend or family member to take some photos of you while you play (not just "still posing"). Another excellent option is have someone videotape your playing (or do your own video set-up). Then watch yourself in the video carefully, focusing only on the way you sit and move and nothing else. Check each part of your body as follows:

A POSTURE CHECKLIST

- ## YOUR HEAD AND NECK POSITION:
  If you are moving your head and pulling your neck forward when trying to read from a score – this will strain the muscles at the bottom of your neck and create tension there in the long run; instead, move your whole upper body forward to facilitate the reading.

- ## YOUR SHOULDERS:
  If they are shrugged most of the time or all the time, or rounded to the front, closing your chest in, these postures are closing your body in and not allowing the energy to flow through your arms down to your hands, fingers, and the piano, thereby making it more difficult for you even without yourself knowing it; instead, open your shoulders and chests to generate energy (and open your heart as well to receive the music from the piano).

- ## YOUR UPPER BODY:
  If it stays upright and is straightened all the way upward from the lower back; if it leans forward, as leaning to the front gives you more energy to channel it down to the piano keys and thus helps to create more sound easily; leaning backward should only occur very occasionally during playing, if at all, for softer passages, for example. Do make sure that when your upper body tilts forward, it is folding at the hip joint rather than rounding the lower back.

- YOUR LOWER BODY:

    If your hip bones are secured firmly down on the bench, your body weight is distributed and balanced evenly to the two sides of your bottom, and that weight can be transferred easily from one side of the bottom to the other when needed – when you have to play notes in the lower register of the keyboard, or the case of the other extreme, the upper register of the keyboard.

BODY AWARENESS EXERCISE: LOWER AND UPPER BODY

Sit on the piano bench, feeling your seat bone set firmly on the bench and your feet grounded heavily on the floor. Fold your upper body from the hip joint, lean forward to the front, then lean farther back from the upright position. Do this motion a few times. Feel the movement of your seat bone when leaning back and forth.

Now try the same leaning movement to the side, first the left side and then the right side. Do not curl your upper body from your waist: it should be moving straight upright and to the sides. You should feel the weight transfer from the left seat bone to the right seat bone and vice versa. Notice that there is a counterbalance of weight between the seat bone and the opposite foot. For example, when you lean to the left side, you should step more on the right foot to stabilize the body, so you do not fall or collapse all the way to the left, and vice versa. You can thus move your arms across the keyboard in the same direction as you move your upper body side to side very consciously.

Counterbalance is the key.

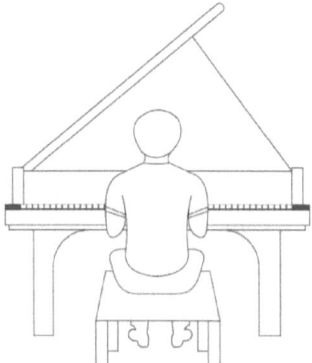

Figure 3a. Middle Position

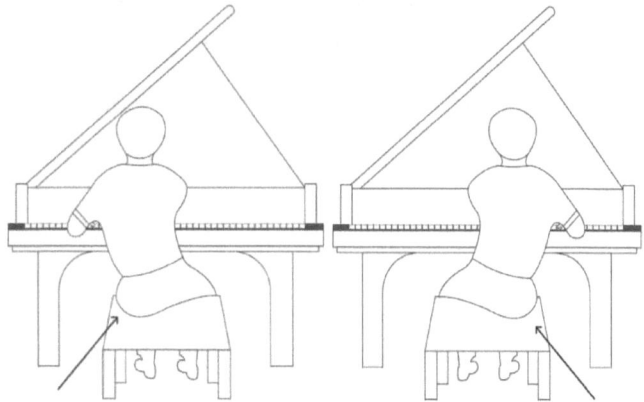

Figure 3b. Leaning to the left side (lower register): push more to the ground with the right foot.

Figure 3c. Leaning to the right side (higher register): push more to the ground with the left foot.

 Watch Technique Transformation Course Video 2: Upper Body Shift.

SHOULDERS

Put your left hand on your left shoulder. Rotate the shoulder blade in one direction, first to the front five times, then the other way to the back another five times.

Feel the shoulder blade and shoulder socket working. Now put your right hand on your right shoulder and repeat this exercise.

Feeling our shoulder blades working is tremendously important. They are the connections between our upper body and our upper arms. This connection helps us deliver both energy and strength to our arms, hands, and fingers.

UPPER ARMS

It is of utmost importance that one keeps the upper arms suspended in the air at all times. I have observed many players keep pushing into the keys without relaxing frequently between attacks, and this constant tightness of the muscles creates a lot of tension in the playing, keeping their playing slow, dragging and harsh sounding, to name just a few negative outcomes.

Keeping your upper arms suspended in the air keeps your fingers and hands light as well, enabling them to go down onto the keys and release them quickly (always velocity before energy, speed before force). Sitting up tall keeps your back straight from the lower back all the way up and helps your upper arms to suspend in the air much more naturally and easily.

A note of caution: keeping your upper arms suspended in the air does not mean they stay at the same height and in the same position all the time. They can move when necessary in fact, they may move a lot, sometimes in a bigger circular motion and at other times a smaller circular motion, depending on what is required for the music. One criterion you can use to judge if your arms are in the right position is that the elbows should never point straight down. Sometimes they can point a little toward the back and a lot of times they will point to either of the two sides. Remember, the music is in constant continuous movement once it starts - even when there are pauses at the rests (these are not exactly rests for the pianist!), so each part of our body must be engaged at all times physically, mentally and emotionally. That engagement includes your upper arms too! Draw more circles with your upper arms and elbows to create smooth phrasing and channel weight transfer down at the piano!

Watch Technique Transformation Course Video 3: Whole Arm Movement and Video 4: Whole Arm Movement II.

FOREARMS

Put your hands on the keyboard, and line up your forearms so that they are parallel to the ground. Isolate the forearms from the upper arms with the elbows as the mid-point. Now try to move only the forearms up and down by folding them from the elbows, locking your wrists, so they are moving with the forearms, not alone.

Hold your upper arms still and close to your upper body. You will feel a lot of tension there, and this is exactly what you do not want in your playing.

Now try to move your forearms side to side while keeping the upper arms locked to your upper body. You can feel there is a limited scope or angle of movement that is generated from the forearms to the elbows only. Notice that such a circular motion is contradictory to the parallel movement we need at the keyboard (because the keyboard runs in a straight line!)

Keep holding the upper arms tight. Now try to move your fingers across the keyboard. Do you find it difficult to do so? Do you feel a lot of tension in the upper arm-shoulder area?

Now release the upper arms from the upper torso, and put the fingers in your natural playing position. Try to expand your arms gradually to the sides by moving your upper arms outward. Feel this movement and the space under the armpits expanding bit by bit when the upper arms are moving out and away from the upper body, and closing in when the upper arms are moving back into the upper body, thereby closing the armpits as well. This motion is what you want in your playing, namely, that the upper arms are free to move in and out so as to support and coordinate with the forearms and hands.

CHAPTER THREE
FINGER-FOREARM ALIGNMENT

As you have learned by now, piano playing is a whole-body action just like playing a sport. You must engage your whole body, so you can fully utilize your body weight to generate the energy you need for your playing. In order to do so successfully, you need to align the fingers independently and accordingly with the forearms, so the energy can flow smoothly and naturally from the body through the whole arm all the way down to each fingertip.

Five-Fingers, Scales, and Arpeggios

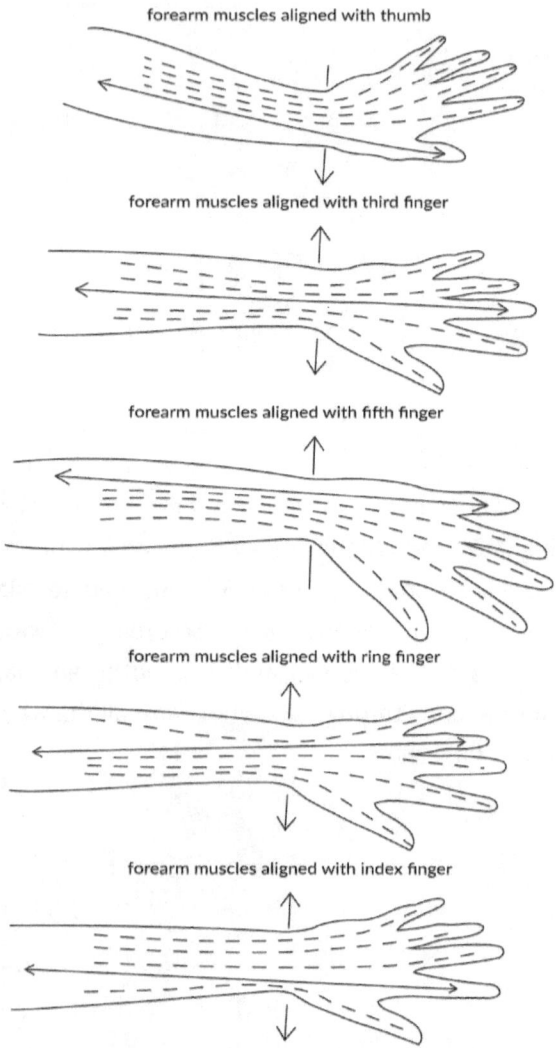

Figure 4. Finger-Forearm Alignment

EXERCISE TIME!

AT THE PIANO: USE C-D-E-F-G-F-E-D-C

Instead of raising each finger high in the air, we move the wrist to the left and right (horizontally) without raising or pulling it down, letting the wrist rise and fall (vertically) ever so slightly and naturally - so that the forearm is aligned with each finger to form a more or less straight line while executing each individual note. Feel the transfer of weight happening under the fingers from the forearm via the wrist. We use a "one-energy" to play all notes in the same phrase or slur by transferring one single attack of weight from the left to the right (thumb to fifth finger in case of the right hand) and vice versa. It is like we have five friends (fingers) playing one ball together by transferring that ball from one end to the other without holding onto the ball ourselves.

The idea is to play comfortably in the most efficient way with the least tension and effort by recycling this "one-energy" back and forth. We need to think more of horizontal movement instead of vertical movement when it comes to phrasing and energy flow at the piano.

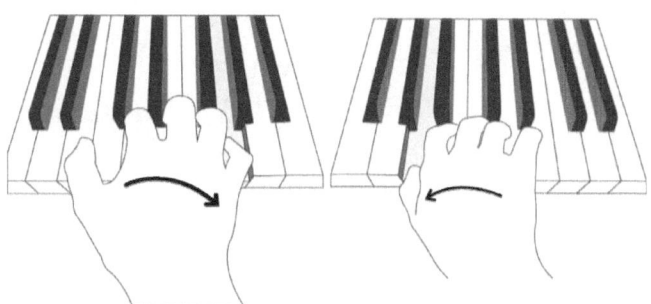

Figure 5. Weight transfer from one finger to another in one hand

HANDS
HAND SHAPE

I find there are equally as many students who have their fingers curl too closely to their palms as those who spread their fingers too widely flat on the keyboard without any support of the palm muscles and knuckles.

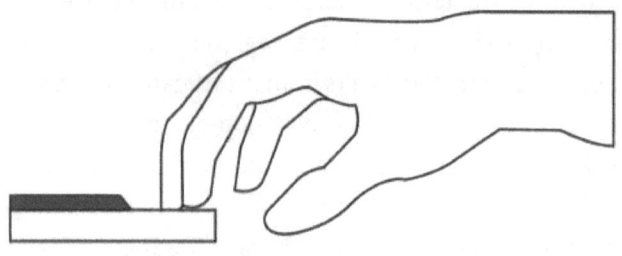

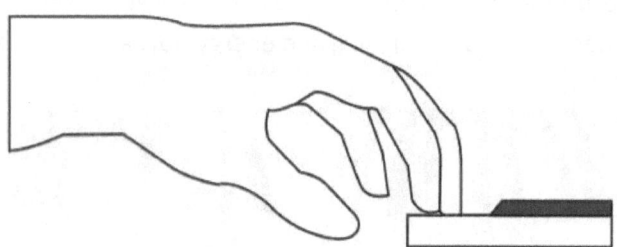

Figure 6. Hand shape and finger knuckles, finger angle (45-60 degree) at the keyboard

PALMS

We must engage the palm to control and move our fingers at the piano. The palm is very powerful. When we activate the palm muscles in our playing, we can apply such techniques as weight transfer and forearm or upper arm rotation more efficiently to present even rhythm at a controlled tempo, whether fast or slow, and create smooth phrasing and tone, whether bright or mellow to our heart's desire.

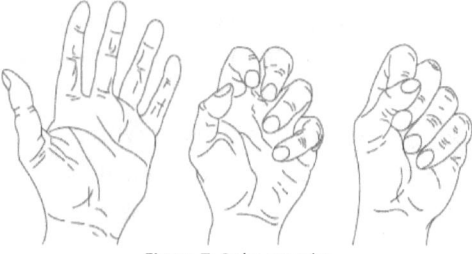

Figure 7. Palm muscles

 Watch Teresa Wong School of Music Video: Strengthening Your Palm Muscles.

EXERCISE TIME!

Squeeze the fingers tightly to make fists. Hold them for five seconds. Then release them to the natural playing position. Do this exercise a few times.

Note: This exercise is intended to let us feel the existence and use of our palm muscles.

(*Yes, we do not feel the existence of our palm muscles and do not use them enough in our playing, as most exercises out there focus on training the fingers but not the bigger muscles or weight transfer.)

WRISTS

It is pretty easy for us to neglect the wrists since the old-school teachers always told us to raise our fingers as high as possible without telling us what to do with our wrists at the same time (not to mention our arms and bodies).

THE POSITION OF THE WRISTS

The wrists should be parallel to the floor, not too high or low, so they can allow the forearms to stay as parallel to the floor as possible.

We should be able to move our wrists up and down; that movement helps us to execute each note clearly and easily without tension. When we strike the keys down (even just one key), the wrists go down immediately right after the attack. After the attack, the wrists go back up to the starting position to release the tension, whether we are still holding the keys down or not.

Let me clarify further about that movement here: This wrist movement comes naturally, meaning that we do not use any force to drag the wrists up and down. In fact, instead of thinking about the wrists, we should think about releasing most of the force and only keeping a minimum amount of that force under the fingers after they have struck the keys down even when still holding the keys. In that way, the wrists can let gravity do its work and go down and up naturally. In terms of the down-up motion, the degree will vary, meaning that there are times the wrists go down and up more and other times they do so less, depending on the duration of the notes and the tempo of the music we are playing, etc.

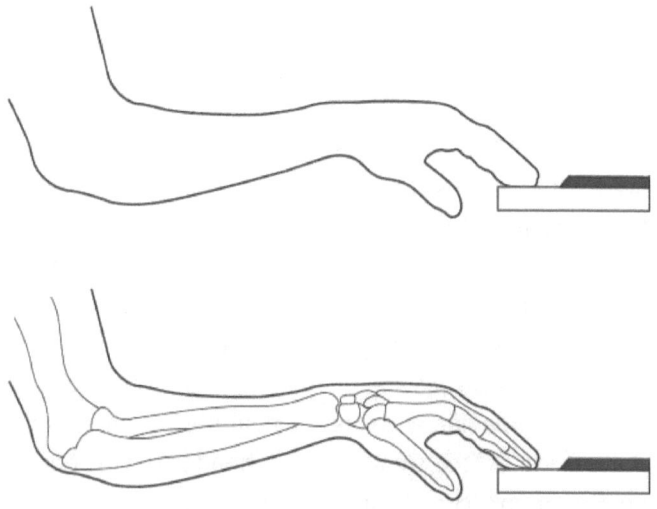

Figure 8. Wrist level parallel to the floor.

 Watch Technique Transformation Course Video 5: Note Clutter and Separate Note Exercise.

EXERCISE TIME!
PART 1

Rotate your wrists in a circle, first clockwise – left to right, then counterclockwise – right to left.

Now close your fingers into your palms to make fists. Move your fists up by folding at the wrists to feel the tension and then down to release that tension.

We have to feel our wrists and understand that they can move in other ways than our fingers can.

EXERCISE TIME!
PART 2

AT THE PIANO: USE C-D-E-F-G-F-E-D-C

Start with the wrist being level and keeping one straight line to the forearm and parallel to the floor. Play each note with a fresh attack (strike and release). Each attack involves the down-up motion, so that when you play C, the wrist bounces a little and goes down along with the attack. When you finish playing C, the wrist bounces back and goes up immediately to the original position right after that attack. Do the same exact motion for D, E, F, and so on. Do this exercise for both hands separately and slowly.

Notice that each execution of a note is based on two beats, so the downward motion is one beat and the upward motion is one beat. Do not move your wrist to let it go up too quickly or abruptly, as that will ruin the purpose of this exercise. Focus on thinking about and keeping your wrist relaxed and flexible---this is the key for achieving the goal of this exercise

The down-up wrist movement is most often applied for a clear separate individual note attack or accent, as well as for short slurs (2-note slurs like those appearing often in classical pieces, and a few note slurs). When we want to connect the notes and create a longer phrase, we keep our wrists stable and calm, but the wrist still goes down at the beginning of the attack on the first note and goes up at the end of the phrase. The down-up movement is also useful for separating different slurred phrases.

 Watch Technique Transformation Course Video 10: Slurs.

FINGERS

I have heard (and indeed experienced myself) that there are teachers who are telling their students to stand their fingers vertically straight, 90 degrees to the keyboard to maintain a good hand position and then strike the keys from high above with much more force, some even with the thumb! (Ouch, that hurts!) Seriously, it does.

With this so-called "finger-independence" technique, we are generating energy with our fingers only without any support or connection with the palm or above (wrist, forearm and upper arm). Believe me when I say this--- it does not work well at all.

Let us first try this experiment to understand what we should not do:

EXPERIMENT

Rest your right hand on a table and maintain a natural playing position, i.e., a round palm with ample space underneath and fingers curved down at the table. Pick up the index finger of your right hand. Pick it up as high as you can, and let it stay up for a few seconds. Do you feel the tension there? You should be feeling some muscle tension under the index finger, particularly right at the bottom of that finger where it joins the palm. Do you feel the tend tendon all the way to the top of your palm where the index finger lies? Now hit the index finger hard on the key, and hold that tension in the finger. Do you feel the tension there as well? This tension is the opposite of what we should feel and do.

The fingers should be a little slanted, or to be precise, somewhere slanted between 45-60 degrees to the keyboard, with all the knuckles out (not indented), especially the first knuckles. The first knuckles are extremely important in supporting our finger stand, so that the attack on the keys delivers a focused energy, and the sound produced has a focused tone as well. When we play, we should feel that there is a focused point under each fingertip, like the tip of a ball pen, indeed a round point that is focused onto the key.

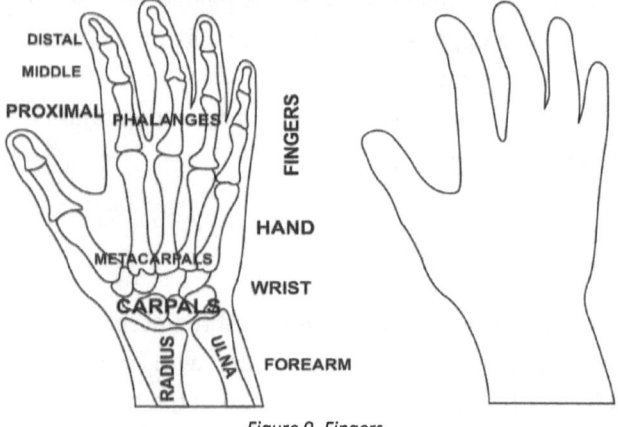

Figure 9. Fingers.

THE ATTACK

The degree of loudness and softness of each note is controlled by the velocity of the attack produced by each finger. To put it more simply, when you want to play louder, play faster onto the keys! By "playing faster" I mean the speed of the finger attacking the key downward (velocity), but not the speed of the note or the piece (rhythm or tempo).

You do need to use a little more energy when you want to play a note louder, but that force is still minimal since it only requires as little as two ounces to press a key down. Think playing faster instead of playing harder. Then after each attack, relax. Release most of the energy. Fingers should stand firm while you release the weight and tension with a minimal force needed to hold the notes down, mainly by gravity (if the notes are longer notes, not staccatos).

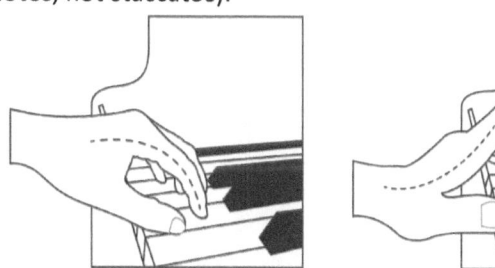

Figure 10. Finger attack right on top of the keys versus from high above.

 Watch Technique Transformation Course Video 5: Note Clutter and Separate Note Exercise.

EXERCISE TIME!

WIGGLE YOUR FINGERS, FEEL THEIR EXISTENCE.

AT THE PIANO: USE C-D-E-F-G-F-E-D-C

Play each note with a fresh attack (strike and release). First experience this attack with the right hand alone. They try it with the left hand alone.

Pay attention to two placements during the exercise:

1. All knuckles out (especially the first finger knuckles and the knuckles that connect the fingers and the palms).
2. Focused point, under the fingertips.

 Watch Technique Transformation Exercise: Ex. 1 (RH - all fingers) & Ex. 1 (LH – all fingers)

THE WEIGHT UNDER THE FINGERS

We want to use the most efficient method that expends the least effort when we play the piano. In order to do so, we have to understand that each attack of a note requires only around two ounces of physical energy, and we cannot alter the sound any further after the attack even if we put more force into that particular finger (Note: we can control or alter the ending sound of a note by the way we release the key and lift our fingers off that key. However, that is another topic for another time.). Therefore, we only need a minimal weight to hold a key down.

It is also important to know that we should transfer a single bolt of energy every time we play a new note. As I mentioned earlier, such a transfer of energy can be compared to the passing of the ball game. In that game there was only one object – the ball – and we needed to pass it between many players. In our piano playing (game) it is the energy (ball) we pass to and through the many notes executed by our fingers (the players).

Every time when you play a note, you should notice whether you are experiencing some tension in your hand after the attack. Notice if there is any tightness in the dorsum of your hand, the upper side that faces the ceiling.

> ** To see how this technique can be achieved and practiced, read more in chapter four.*

CHECKPOINT

For me, the ideal sitting position at the piano is having my feet somewhat wider than my hips, with my thighs parallel to the floor and my knees forming 90 degrees, and no squeezing between them. I can then stand up from the piano bench at any time, feeling my weight solidly grounded on the floor. Sometimes I will move my left foot farther out when I am reaching for the lower bass register and respectively my right foot farther out also to reach for the higher upper register, so that I will gain more support and energy in my playing from my whole body. I also like to sit a little lower at the bench in order to apply the principle of leverage to the keys. My wrists and forearms form a straight line with each another when not playing, and my forearms stay slightly slanted to the floor, allowing me to use the body weight transferred from my upper body through my shoulders and upper arms. Some pianists may prefer a higher sitting position to feel more weight on the keyboard due to a smaller build. Most importantly, you have to find your own comfortable position, which allows you to use your body freely for the most efficient, engaging, and powerful playing.

Watch Technique Transformation Course Video 1: Sitting Posture and Body Weight Shift.

CHAPTER FOUR
THE "THINK BIG" EXERCISE

The following is a general checklist you can follow every time before you practice. I call it the "think big" exercise:

Figure 11. Sitting posture at the piano

- Start thinking about the big picture: Your posture.
- Think about your seat bones firmly situated on the piano bench. Your feet are securely grounded to the floor, the distance between them being somewhat wider than your hips. In this position you can move your body from side to side, transferring the body weight from left seat bone to right seat bone, and from right seat bone back to left seat bone.
- Think about straightening your back, starting slowly from your lower back, then moving gradually up to your mid-back, and finally your upper back.
- Think and feel your body weight. Is it in the middle, to the front or the back of your torso? Try to keep it more to the front, and do not lean back, so there will be more support and body connection to your arms, hands, and fingers, making it easier to move and play.
- Think about your shoulders: I have noticed many students have this problem of rounding their shoulders in and forward. Broaden your shoulders out and to the side. Open up your chest, your heart moving towards the piano. Relax your shoulders down instead of shrugging them and tensing them upwards. Feel the connection from your shoulder blades and shoulder joint sockets, and channel the energy down to your arms, hands and fingers.
- Think about activating your upper arms to provide support to your forearms, which are commonly and easily abused by too much tightening of one set of their muscles and no releasing and transferring of the energy.

- Think about your fingers' connections to your palms and your wrists. Fingers tend to be over-activated (due to all those "finger independence" exercises misused by many students, or given to abuse other students) and this over-activity can cause tension in the palms, wrists, and forearms. *
- Think big--- think motion of the whole body, not just small movement by the fingers.
- Think broad--- think heavy round sound, not small, acute, harsh, and thin sound.
- Start today: Think big, use your big muscles, and make big sound.

CHAPTER FIVE

THE TRANSFER OF WEIGHT – BERNSTEIN'S WEIGHT TRAINING METHOD

The truth is that it is not what we have not done with our playing, but rather what we have been doing too much to hinder great playing from happening.

The first thing we always notice is the way we execute the notes with our fingers, which have the closest connection from our body to the keyboard. However, it is not about how high we raise our fingers or how hard we move our fingers down to strike the keys, but rather how we play most efficiently with ease using the least energy. Simply put, when we want to play more efficiently and effectively, it is about speed (velocity) – how fast or slow we strike the keys with our fingers – rather than the force (weight) – how hard or soft we strike them.

Let us think about running for a moment. When we run, do we pick up our legs and feet very high every step we take? (Only true if we are acting in a silly comedy movie!) Instead of picking up our legs and feet awkwardly high, we pick them up only high enough to keep our running pace smooth, steady, and fast. In that manner, the way we run will be continuous, non-stop and smoothly flowing.

Figure 12. Running.

This is pretty easy to imagine and understand. Now let's try walking.

Think about the way we walk. When we walk normally, are our moves continuous and smooth in a constant, steady pace? Is every movement in our walking a similar distance and speed? Do our legs and feet move in a continuous flow, so that they never stop in between our movements during our walk unless we stop?

If you are not sure, try walking now and notice your movement.

EXERCISE TIME!

Stand up and find an area where you can walk straight ahead for about five normal-distance steps that are your own. Now start walking rather slowly. Pick up your right foot and start walking to the front. Right-left-right-left-right-left. Now turn and walk again. Left-right-left-right-left-right. Do you notice that when you are walking toward the front with your right foot, your left foot is already halfway off the ground, and vice versa?

Now walk again. This time notice the way you are moving your legs and feet. Do you find that your legs and feet do not stop completely in between every step you take? That means that in order to walk smoothly, our legs and feet must stay in constant smooth motion, always adjusting their movement, even between the steps we take.

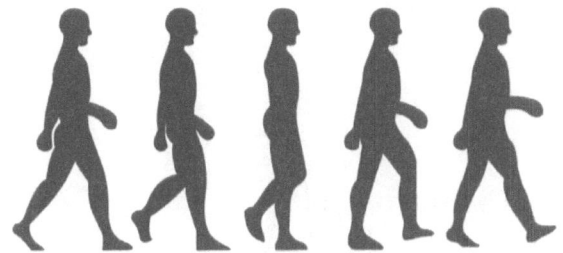

Figure 13. Walking with motion.

Now let's do something really silly.

Pick up your feet one by one. Notice that the movement is generated from the feet, but not the legs. Tighten your legs and lock your knees, so that you feel like they are almost immobile. Now try to walk a straight line this way. Do you find that your steps are smaller than those you made before? Do you notice that you are walking rather silly like a child or a penguin would?

Figure 14. Walking with the legs tight.

Let's try something even more ridiculous.

Pick up your right foot and stand with all your bodyweight on your left foot. Now try walking toward the front with all the weight on the left leg and foot. Can you walk smoothly? Do you find that your left leg is very heavy while your right leg is very light, thus making it extremely difficult to move forward?

Figure 15. Walking with the weight on one side.

This series of experiments tells us that in order to walk far and smoothly, we need to use the bigger muscles (our legs) to let the smaller muscles (our feet) produce a continuous flow. We also need to transfer our weight from side to side (left and right) in order to move forward easily and efficiently.

How about the other way? Try walking by picking up each leg one after the other as high as your hip joint, to form a 90-degree angle with the other leg, as though you are marching. Is that efficient? Is it fast and easy?

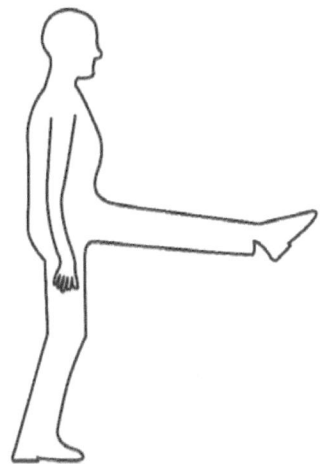

Figure 16. Walking with thigh up high at 90 degrees

WHAT DO ALL THESE EXERCISES HAVE TO DO WITH OUR PLAYING?

The principle of playing with our fingers is similar to the principle of walking with our legs.

We do not walk by picking up our feet and putting them extremely high in the air. Then why would we do the same thing with our fingers raised and then hit the keys from high above the keyboard?

We use not only our feet, but also our legs – thighs and calves to walk far distances. Then why would we only use our fingers, but not our arms – forearms and upper arms – to help our fingers move across the keys?

We move our legs and feet in a smooth and continuous motion to walk forward. Why not do the same with our fingers and arms when we play the piano?

We need to transfer our weight from one foot to the other to move our body forward. Why do we not practice the same transfer of weight from one finger to another?

We do not tense our legs and feet when we walk. Why do we tense our fingers and wrists and keep our arms tightened close to the body when we play?

If we want our playing to sound smooth, we must move smoothly. We must transfer the weight from one finger to another to use our energy in the most economical manner. We do need to pick up our fingers, but only so high that we can strike with velocity (not force) for great volume and a brilliant (not harsh) tone.

Now let's see how we can train our fingers to feel the keys. Below is a revolutionary method that has changed the way I play forever.

BERNSTEIN'S WEIGHT TRAINING METHOD

Years ago, I encountered an amazing book. It was called Seymour Bernstein's *With Your Own Two Hands.*

Bernstein is a prolific composer, pianist, and much sought-after piano pedagogue in the United States. He also keeps himself busy with writing, primarily on the subject of piano playing. *With Your Own Two Hands* is certainly a great work on that topic. It is a wonderful read: it covers everything from piano teaching to piano practice and performance. Its tone is both compassionate and genuine that the readers can truly feel the sincerity of the author, who happily shares without any reservation at all his own learning experiences, teaching philosophy, and methods.

The best thing I ever learned from this book is the use of arm weight (or simply "body weight" in extension). The method of weight training introduced by Bernstein revolutionized my way of playing, and it has given me amazing freedom on the keyboard, indeed a freedom that I have never experienced before, and this freedom has stayed with me to the present. I am greatly indebted to the practice. So much so, that I now want to share with all the magic and beauty of this method with you.

This weight training method is presented in Bernstein's book, Chapter Seven: "You and the Piano", under the section "Arm Weight". In the chapter, Bernstein talks about his early experience using weights for piano practice when he was sixteen. Supplied by his father, Bernstein had small steel balls and sewed them between two leather pieces. He then attached the pieces around his wrist and started to practice at the piano. Using this experiment, he immediately felt the sensation of heavy weight from the arms and the fingertips to the keyboard and delivered less effort, more control of touch and better projection of sound and tone.

Bernstein suggested using the weight straps found in athlete supplies stores at one to five pounds of weight. So during my graduate study at Indiana University, I found a sporting good store and bought a couple of weight straps of around three to five pounds each with magnetic stripes. They were originally for leg training and were to be strapped around the ankles. I strapped them around my wrists instead.

I followed Bernstein's suggestion very strictly so as not to hurt my hands. At first I started by using one weight strap around my wrists alternately and with each hand practicing for no more than five minutes. Initially the weight was very heavy on the wrist, but I instantly felt the difference under my fingers and also in the sounds I heard as I produced them on the piano.

After a while I got used to it, and I started to extend the practice time to a longer period of ten to fifteen minutes. I also compared the difference in my feelings between using the weights and not using them. I found that once I got used to having weights on my wrist, there was much more feeling of the weight under the fingers on the keys, more control of the touch and the sound I produced, and thus more freedom in my playing, even later when I was not strapping the weights around my wrists. I also used both weights on the wrists at the same time to work on not only the sensation of weight, but also the weight transfer. With the weight I also trained myself the five major technical patterns on their own, which I discuss in the next chapter - as well as applying them in the musical pieces I was working on. I also limited the duration of each weighted practice to no more than fifteen minutes to protect my hands.

For those of my readers who truly want to adopt a new way of playing and use weight instead of force, you should definitely try this experiment. Just try playing at the piano with the weights on your wrists. You will immediately feel the difference. Nonetheless, you must be very careful with such weight training. First of all, do not fight against the weight. Let the weight sink naturally onto your arms and wrists, so you can feel the heaviness under your fingertips right down to the keys. Second, use a lighter weight, e.g. three pounds, or even just one pound to start with. Also, begin practicing with one weight on one wrist first for a couple of minutes, then put one weight on the other wrist for another couple minutes. Practice with scales or even just five notes moving back and forth (C-D-E-F-G and G-F-E-D-C). It is not important what you practice with; it is rather the weight you feel in your fingertips and the transfer of weight from one finger to another. It is like tai-chi where there is only "one-energy" and that energy is flowing back and forth, left and right. Always go slow when you start a new practice such as this one. Take your time to feel the sensation and the movement before practicing at a faster speed.

Notice also that when we say weight transfer, that means there is only one weight being used and being transferred from one finger to another. For instance, when you are playing with your index finger of the right hand, you only feel all the weight under the index finger down to the key, while all the other fingers are quite light and relaxed. Then, when you play with the middle finger next, the weight will completely transfer away from the index finger, which is now relaxed. You can stand on the middle finger under which the weight is transferred down to the key being held by the fingertip. There should be little tension under the finger and in the hand. Remember, firmness and strength are very different technical aspects from tension and tightness. Indeed, only a fraction of energy is necessary to hold one finger on the key and keep the sound sustained when required.

Watch Technique Transformation Exercise Series: Ex 1: Training with Weights (LH/RH).

CHECKPOINT

For all the experiments offered in this and the following chapters, please do try them, but one by one slowly with the utmost patience and focus. Observe each of your movements very carefully.

Analyze and enlarge every little detail, like you would with a microscope. Practice each exercise with both focus and confidence.

Trust that each experiment and exercise is helping you move one step closer toward gaining full freedom in your piano playing. Only by applying that kind of faith and self-confidence will this book work for you.

CHAPTER SIX
SÁNDOR'S FIVE BASIC MOTIONS OF PIANO TECHNIQUE

So far, I have covered quite a lot about the physiological condition of the human body and the application of the individual bodily parts in our piano playing. Another important question, however, should be raised now: Why do we need technique at all in our piano playing?

Piano technique is a crucial tool and one that a pianist has to acquire to be serious about playing the piano. It is a technique that helps the player understand perfectly and clearly how to execute the musical notes with different combination of actions in specific parts of the arms (the fingers, wrists, forearms, upper arms, even the shoulder blades) with the supporting movement and weight from the whole body (upper body and lower body), so that the movement not only enhances one's playing, but also provides the player with an efficient and effective way to produce the desired sound and tone quality with ease.

I understand that some students (or even teachers) will say, 'What is all this nonsense about? We play with emotion!" Indeed, many students believe that playing the piano is all about feeling and emotion, and therefore, they just go with the flow. They are reluctant to learn, address and practice all the technical issues I present here.

I was once like my students, thinking that one should play with the heart and the soul, and there was nothing rational about the process. I played with passion. I thought I was supposed to feel really tired and painful after I practiced a lot, as that result meant I worked hard and played with great effort to perfect the music. I also thought I needed to feel tired and sense pain to express how much work I was putting into my art.

For me, technique sounded too "scientific", and contradictory to making music. (I felt the same toward computer technology back then, but look at me and the world today!) Indeed, gradually I found that even with practicing many hours per day I was not achieving the progress I had expected, so I began to wonder if my way of practicing countless numbers of hours without specific methods would really improve my playing in the long run. I started going to the library and looking for "piano technique" books. I found plenty of them, indeed an overflow on the subject provided by different writers. In addition to the one I discussed in the last chapter (Bernstein's), there is another one I found tremendously useful and practical for clearly understanding and developing excellent piano techniques in great detail. If there is only one book on piano technique one should read, this is it.

For an inexhaustible and comprehensive resource for any pianist and piano teacher who wants to understand the details of "piano technique", I highly recommend *On Piano Playing: Motion, Sound and Expression* by György Sándor, himself a great pianist and indeed a student of Béla Bartók.

Although the language is not difficult, and the writing is simple with clear ideas, this book is not an elementary manual for beginners and players at graded levels. Students with a higher level of proficiency at piano playing – at least at performance level and undergraduates getting a piano major or above – will find it challenging and yet fascinating to read.

First and foremost, I'll quote a passage offering a bit of Sándor's sage advice here to start:

"Our main concern is not the unsuccessful performances that result from these wrongs, but all the damage caused during the countless hours, weeks and years spent practicing. How much discomfort and suffering we must put up with! They can and must be avoided, especially since pianists have an enormous repertoire to cope with, larger than any other instrumentalists, and cannot afford to waste time and energy on wrong practice habits. With all the frustrations of strenuous practicing, many pianists become either discouraged or obsessive about proving themselves and will make a virtue of punishing themselves in the name of Art. It is for this reason that many people poured into it. My apologies for sounding glib, but I wish merely to make the point that the mechanics of piano playing ought to be completely painless, enjoyable, and gratifying whether one practices or concertizes." (p.6)

FIVE BASIC MOTIONS

Sándor identifies five basic technical patterns for piano playing. He lists them in the following order:

1. Free fall
2. Five-fingers, scales and arpeggios
3. Rotation
4. Staccato
5. Thrust

Let's start with the five-fingers pattern.

FIVE-FINGERS, SCALES, AND ARPEGGIOS

Some of us are all too familiar with the five-fingers patterns, as well as scales and arpeggios, from all the graded exams from England (Associated Board of the Royal Schools of Music, ABRSM or Trinity College of Music) that we have taken in Hong Kong and other Asian countries (also obviously in England, while Australia and Canada have their own slightly different but similar exam board systems). I do notice it is not that common to take exams in the United States and Europe, where their systems are completely different. But that is another story and shall be told another time.

I would like to clarify here that scales are indeed not only essential for passing an exam, but also crucial for developing the pianist technique. We can find patterns of scales and arpeggios in all kinds of repertoires. If we are familiar with the scales and their respective fingerings, we can sight read a song much more quickly and learn it more easily by being able to identify these familiar patterns.

Many have mistaken piano technique for something you simply gain by practicing repeated patterns mindlessly, using same old tedious finger exercises thousands of times. Yet listen to what a great pianist like Sándor has to say about this viewpoint:

"Independence of the fingers is essential; but instead of trying to acquire it by forced and muscle-stiffening exercises, our fundamental approach to technical solutions is to search for the correct positions in which the right equipment helps the finger work independently and provides them with the power they need." (p.17)

I could not agree more. Many of us who have tried to work on the strength and independence of our fingers have experienced, after hours of practice, fatigue or even pain from overstrained muscles. It is not because our muscles are weak, so we must keep training them until they become strong. As Sándor explains, it is rather that we need to know the correct use of muscles and the coordination required in order to gain full mobility in our hands and freedom in our playing.

"[T]he aligning and adjusting [of the fingers] should be continuous and exact." (p.55)

Here I would emphasize the word "continuous" since many times the problem does not lie in no adjustment, but rather in a jerky and abrupt, angular way of adjustment.

The alignment and structure of our fingers undeniably determines how we should use them.

We need to learn how to use our fingers effectively to get the best results. Each finger, except for the thumb, has three segments for which the technical term is "phalanxes". Therefore, the thumb, which has two phalanxes, requires special attention and plays in a different position than do the other four fingers. In fact, each finger should be played with a slight adjustment due to its different alignment to the forearm. However, the thumb is structured in an entirely different position that is alien to the other fingers so that subject is discussed separately. (To read more about the thumb, see Chapter Five of Sándor's book.)

I have heard some teachers advocate that students play with the first phalanx of the thumb straight and vertical to the keys. How wrong that idea is, as it will hurt the thumb by putting it in a completely unnatural position!

How about the fingers other than thumb? For these digits, Sándor writes:

"While the other four fingers differ distinctly from the thumb, they also vary among themselves. They differ in shape and size and, although they have adequate muscles, they are not equal in length." (p.58)

Therefore, we need to provide constant adjustment for the different fingers.

Many piano learners often find themselves in a difficult position when utilizing the fourth and fifth fingers and especially the fifth fingers, which are considered by many as the "weak" ones. In fact, this is not true.

First let us read what Sándor says about the fourth finger:

"The fourth finger, in particular, feels weak, but not because it lacks strong muscles. However, the flexors and extensors are wrapped together with the third finger's muscles: hence these two fingers tend to contract and extend together. The fourth finger cannot be totally independent of the third. But it is possible to make the horizontal and vertical adjusting motions so precise, so accurate that activation of the fourth finger can be done effortlessly." (p.58)

Especially the beginners, or even the more seemingly advanced students, have been wrongly informed with the false notion that the solution to the "independence" of the fingers is the mindless drill of "strengthening" exercises. However, they should understand why these two fingers seem to be stuck together.

What about the fifth fingers? To that, Sándor writes:

"Contrary to common belief the fifth finger is one of the strong fingers...in addition to the forearm muscles; it has a special set of strong muscles at the outer side of the hand... It certainly needs this strength since most of the fundamental bass notes are played by the left and the melodies by the right hand's fifth fingers, as well as most of the "virtuoso" octave passages." (p.59)

If we activate the palm muscles that are connected to the fifth fingers instead of raising the fingers alone when playing, we would soon discover these fingers are in fact strong and powerful.

EXERCISE TIME!

START WITH YOUR RIGHT HAND.

Place your left index finger on the joint of your right fifth finger, where that finger is connected to the palm.

Now isolate the fifth finger from the joint connected to the palm and raise that finger up.

Can you sense that the movement of the fifth finger is mostly initiated from the joint, but not really connected much to the palm and the arm?

Next, raise the fifth finger high up in the air and freeze it by activating the outer side of your right palm. The action is so swift and precise that you would feel your forearm rotating inward to your body while your elbow is moving to the outside, away from your upper torso. Your thumb should also feel the movement, so it would shift a little downward and to the right (outward) as well. Now you execute a note (any note) by attacking with your fifth finger moving down as fast as possible. You should feel that your upper arm is working (going down and in toward your upper torso), your forearm is rotating outward (in a clockwise direction), and your elbow is moving in toward your body.

You can also try the same exercise with your left hand.

CHECKPOINT

Training the fifth fingers is of tremendous significance because, as stated by Sándor, we need them to project the melodies on the top line and the bass line. Also, awakening and activating the outer palm muscles that are connected to the fifth fingers can increase our awareness of our hand and palm muscle control and let us play chords with solid resonance.

This five-finger technique is often applied in scalic patterns or modified scalic passages.

Watch Technique Transformation Course Video 5: Note Clutter and Separate Note Exercise, Video 10: Slurs, Video 11: Scales, Video 12: Chromatic Scales, Video 13 Arpeggios, and Ex 1: RH individual fingers 3, 4, 5

ROTATION

It is also essential to understand the anatomy of the arm, since the fingers cannot stand on their own and play by themselves. (I always use the example of the chopped hand in the box in the classic movie, *The Addams Family* to illustrate this point – that chopped hand can move independently on its own while ours cannot!) The fingers are controlled by the hand (the palm muscle), the wrist, and the forearm, with strong support from the upper arm and upper back (shoulder blades). If we keep abusing the smaller muscles (our fingers) without activating and connecting to the stronger muscles (forearm, upper arm and back), we will get tired easily and even hurt ourselves after hours of practice.

The upper side of the forearm – the extensor muscles – contracts while the lower side of the arm – the flexor muscles – relaxes. It is thus the constant alternate tightening and relaxing of these two sets of muscles that allow the forearm to generate power to the fingers without feeling strained. When we have acquired this appropriate use of the forearm, we can avoid the first cause of fatigue, * the muscular tension that usually occurs in the forearm and the overstraining of one particular set of muscles.

> *Some players even get tension in their hands due to the fact that they are not using their palm muscles properly to control the fingers, so they can move in a more precise fashion.*

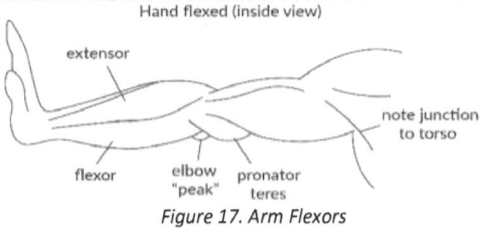
Figure 17. Arm Flexors

WHEN DO WE USE ROTATION?

We use rotation basically at all times whenever we play a melodic line with steps and skips up and down especially in legato fashion (even when it is in staccato articulation there is rotation in the staccato phrase). Its application is definitely more noticeable in those passages with broken-chord figurations, such as Alberti bass and arpeggios, melodic lines with bigger intervallic leaps, as well as in scale-like passages.

Notice that the degree of rotation should be larger and more exaggerated when applied in passages of bigger leaps (e.g., when playing a bigger melodic interval of a 6th or even an octave, you should rotate your forearm more than for a 2nd or 3rd), as well as when playing a slower tempo.

Remember, the main principle is that we use weight transfer in our playing and the rotation movement is to facilitate such weight transfer. The rotation movement also helps create a long flowing musical phrase in a legato singing style.

> *Note: To understand more about this topic, please read Chapter Three of Sándor's book, "The Human Performing Mechanism".*

 Watch Technique Transformation Course Video 8: Weight Transfer and Oscillating Octaves, Video 13: Arpeggios, and Video 14: Trills.

STACCATO

"In scales and arpeggios and in rotation, most muscular activities take place within the forearm area, and they are helped, actively or passively, by the upper arm. However, in the staccato motion the entire arm, including the upper arm, is actively engaged at all times." (p.93)

Sándor writes here that staccato technique is the same for the staccatos of single notes, double notes, chords and even octaves although I would add that playing single notes does involve more wrist movement and less upper arm movement.

It is not easy to notice how the arm is involved in this technique. To start:
- First, focus on the lower part of the palm movement (down and up).
- Then, notice if the upper arm is restrained or tightened.

The involvement of the upper arm is significant, but the degree of its motion is smaller in comparison to the motion at the wrist.

Note that when the playing is slow, the degree of motion is larger and more noticeable. Therefore, when the playing becomes faster, the degree of motion is smaller and less noticeable. However, you have to make sure that the movement is still there, namely, that the upper arm is still working, but not locked to the upper torso.

Most do believe that in order to play staccato notes, one must hold the wrist down, lock it, and then pick up the fingers quickly. This technique is wrong. Contrary to this action, one should hop the fingers off the keys lightly, or rather, lift the fingers off from the keys with that action generated all the way from the upper arm, so that the wrist re-bounces (down a little) and then up into the air, and the wrist becomes higher than the fingers. The fingers should only be just a little off the keys; they need not be sprung particularly high in the air, so they are relaxed following the staccato action.

It is similar to when one wants to jump in the air: one pushes the feet into the ground in order to go higher into the air, and the knees are soft and not locked the whole time (even when in the air). Then knees can serve as a shock-absorbing mechanism when the feet do come down to the ground again. The same goes for the fingers, namely, when they are pushed up in the air away from the keys, the knuckles are relaxed and not tensed.

Imagine that the keyboard is a trampoline. You hop the fingers like you are jumping off the trampoline up and down, up and down. Or imagine your fingers are like rabbits: they can hop lightly at the trampoline and off to the grasslands in the forest.

Figure 18. Trampoline and Rabbit

 Watch Technique Transformation Course Video 9: Wrist Staccatos.

FREE FALL AND THRUST

Of all the five motion techniques, I find it most difficult to explain these two techniques and their concepts, but I will try my best here.

FREE FALL

Free fall is all about gravity.

As I repeatedly say to my students, it only requires two ounces of pressure to hold a key down.

So what is all the fuss about hitting a key so hard with so much force and continuing to hold it with ever tightening fingers and arms?

Although free fall uses gravity, that does not mean we do not have to do anything as we play. We still have to play the right keys at the right time. That means we have to control the use of gravity correspondingly.

According to Sándor, there are three steps in this free fall technique:

Lift, drop, and land and rebound.

1. LIFT

When we think about the term "lift", it is obvious that we have to lift something up. However, we also have to lift in the following order: from the upper arm, then the forearm, followed by the hands, and finally, the fingers.

There should be a distance for the fingers to drop to the keyboard. Sándor suggests around ten inches. I don't think one needs to measure the distance too precisely, thus, estimating approximately that distance from above the keyboard, as Sándor suggests, will be just fine.

Another detail to notice is that the joints – meaning the shoulder joints, elbows, wrists, and finger knuckles – should be "resilient and firm", plus be "fixed only at the instant the finger depresses the key" (p.42).

> *Note: To be "resilient" means to recover quickly from a changed shape or action. In this case, the term means that the joints should go back into their original condition before the fall and remain relatively relaxed and flexible, rather than loose or flabby. The word "resilient" is thus a much more precise word to describe the action than the term "flexible".*

2. DROP

The dropping step is in fact much more passive than the other two steps: the lifting and rebounding in the whole free fall process.

You should feel your whole arm, hand, and fingers becoming completely relaxed right after the drop. Pay special attention to that feeling in your slow practice of the technique, as it is the most difficult part of the whole action to get right.

3. LAND AND REBOUND

Here is when the keys are executed and the notes sound.

"This fixation causes the transference of energy into the keys and a slight rebound of the hand and fingers, and notably, of the wrist." (p.42)

"A very important detail to watch out for is that the wrist must be in a relatively low position at landing, so that it can cushion naturally." ^(pp .42-3)

It is easy to notice if the wrist is doing the work by watching its vertical movement. In terms of the upper arm and even the shoulder muscle, you will have to feel their movement. That is why it was essential to introduce the seemingly strange body movement in the second chapter.

Feeling the movement of your upper body parts is the first big step, to apply that movement and the feeling of it into your playing is yet a completely different task.

Nonetheless, with lots of patience, time and effort, and a clear focus on the awareness of feeling in the body and the practice of the movement, your playing will advance greatly in the long run.

WHEN DO WE USE A FREE FALL?

Gravity works on its own terms, distance is given for acceleration, and insufficient speed will be generated in any free fall without the addition of a throw. Therefore, we can only employ free fall in those passages of a moderate tempo. Nothing can "drop fast"!

I would also add that we use free fall for big-sounding chords or octaves with longer duration (note value) in music of a slower tempo, as we need more time to generate the action, certainly time that we do not have when playing fast-paced passages or pieces.

THRUST

To quote Sándor once more:

"We place the fingers right on the surface of the keys and push the keys down with a sudden instantaneous contraction of some of the strongest body and arm muscles (the chest, stomach, back triceps and forearm flexor muscles). This action generates maximum speed in the fingertips." (p.108)

"In this thrust, unlike the techniques described before, the fingers are in constant contact with the keys; they touch the keys before, during and after the actual sudden muscle contraction takes place." (p.108)

"The fingers stay on the surface of the keys, and the arms are slightly bent." (p.109)

Do you clearly understand this technique? Let me give you an example:

Think about playing a ball game, for example, either badminton or volleyball. There is a ball coming from the other side and it is high in the air, and you want to get it really badly.

So you have to jump unusually high to get to that ball. Now you are standing with your feet grounded on the floor. In order to get to that unbelievable height, you must push your feet into the floor so you can spring from that floor and get to the ball.

That push is the thrust like your fingers to the keys - except your fingers do not leave the keys after the push.

The push is, as Sándor describes it, an "instantaneous" action. To push your fingers into the keys, you must use your upper body, especially your chest muscles and arm muscles. Notice whether the triceps (the back muscles of your upper arms) are working. When you push your fingers into the keys and execute the notes, you will feel your upper body also moving back at the same time, like a rebounding. It is as if you are pushing yourself away from something scary or someone you are absolutely angry with, so that your whole person is moving back, bouncing in the opposite direction from where you pushed. You should be able to feel that momentum.

WHAT ARE THE DIFFERENCES BETWEEN FREE FALL AND THRUST?

1. You use free fall with your fingers dropping down to the keys from high above and pushing away from the keys after the execution of the notes. With thrust, your fingers always stay on the keys, both before and after the keys are struck.
2. Free fall is all about gravity. You do not have to push. You just need to have your hand position ready and let your arms fall. The speed of the action is slower. For thrust, however, you have to push with great speed and in a split second. You do need to use more force in this action.

3. Free fall can create a much louder sound, as the velocity of the action becomes much stronger. Thrust, on the other hand, can be applied to produce a smaller sonority like medium loud or even a soft sound.
4. Free fall is more suitable for easier chords with fewer notes, e.g., octaves and regular chord patterns. Thrust should be applied on more extended chords with more notes and complicated harmony to provide more security about getting the notes right.

Watch Technique Transformation Course Video 15: Thrust and Free Fall.

CHAPTER SEVEN
MY METHODOLOGY

Having discussed the methods Bernstein and Sándor offer, you are now probably asking yourself – what about my method?

First of all, a new method cannot be invented out of nowhere. It must be a combination of the essence of the great existing methods, as well as the creation of innovative ideas. I have learned much from all the great pianists and writers who have contributed tremendously to helping me develop my own technique. These have been described, especially in Chapters Four and Five. I also gained my basic understanding of human anatomy in Chapters Two and Three from Mr. Sándor's monumental work, but the idea of body awareness exercises is 100% my own creation.

When I was young, I did not appreciate the value of piano technique. Instead, I despised the idea of developing it, misinterpreting the process as merely the vanity of sheer showmanship. I was very wrong. Without proper technique, a pianist will not go very far. One's ideas cannot be expressed, even when one is very musical. The hands alone cannot bring out the essence of sheer beauty of the music one is feeling and the ideas in one's head and heart. Tightened muscles always desert the hard-working music-loving pianist.

Piano technique is the tool to achieve the realization of a pianist's musical ideas that come from the heart and the mind and through the hands.

My method has a very simple concept. Start your training with your mind, and then use your mind to train your hands. An always remember-- your mind controls your hands.

Believe me, you can control those hands. Just think you can, believe you can, and it will happen.

Do not ever let yourself say, "Oh, but I cannot change the way I think". Start today to use your brain and your willpower. Think positive, imagine new possibilities, and always stay confident. Change the way you play by trying out new methods (e.g., mine offered here). Do not be afraid of change or taking a risk. It is constant trial and error that has helped me change the way I play. Yet it was no easy task, so I had to give myself enough time and effort to succeed. Remember, I was playing the five-note exercise— C-D-E-F-G-F-E-D-C – single-hand and repeatedly to get the technique I needed during my first year of graduate study in the States! So if I did it, you can, too.

Do not be afraid to work at exercises that may seem silly at first. They are very useful in getting the proper technique, and you will realize their value after you work on them for a while.

When you are working on a complex piece like a Chopin Ballade or Étude, there is not much time left to focus on one small, precise hand movement. You cannot develop a new technique that way.

To work on improving my technique, I used the weight training method introduced by Bernstein. I wrapped the weight on my wrist and practiced the five-finger exercise (as described above) to begin my daily practice, starting with five minutes every day, then slowly, diligently, and gradually extending the duration to ten minutes or longer. At first, I was not sure if this weight training exercise would work. I could only feel the pressure on my fingers with the weights, and even a little less without them. I was very focused on this simple exercise, feeling just the slightest difference in my playing and the transfer of weight among my fingers. I started to feel more of my arms and my body weight and immediately made use of them.

There was no certainty that Bernstein's weight training exercise would work for me, however I just kept trying, and finally it did wonders to my playing. (Read more of the details in Chapter Four.)

Of course I did practice my regular repertoire along with this exercise. Also, I used the weight to practice a Chopin Ballade or Concerto. Practicing solely on the technique of the exercise is necessary, but you also have to apply that technique to playing your own repertoire as well. You have to do both in order to improve your technique in a significant way.

I am also not trying to argue that this is the only method you can apply to improve your technique, but I tried it and it worked great for me. For sure I would not be writing this book if I had never tried this method, which became a conglomerate of ideas by Bernstein, Sándor as well as myself. I can assure you that I read countless books on piano methods and technique before I found these two, and I did not gain much from the others. I sincerely encourage you to try them out, using patience, focus, diligence and persistence and apply both time and effort in them.

The increased awareness of our bodies is instrumental in improving our playing and applying the changes in our piano technique spontaneously and almost instantly.

It is not that we do not know the existence of the body, but we just do not pay much attention to it. Have you ever noticed the way your arms move, toward and away from the upper torso, the straightness or curviness of the unseen horizontal line these body parts (and your hands) make when up your fingers are going up and down at the keyboard? How do your upper arms move at the shoulder during your playing? And when your fingers strike the keys, do they go up and down in a straightforward motion, or are you in fact pulling them in toward you or pushing them out during and/or after your attack on the keys? When you pay more attention to such tiny little details, you will be very surprised to learn details you have never noticed before but still have been around for years and hindering you from playing better.

Never overlook or ignore the little details, as they are the ones that really count, especially when it comes to polishing your piano technique.

CHAPTER EIGHT
PRACTICE MAKES PERFECT: ONLY IF YOU KNOW HOW

Practice is the essential bridge that links between lesson and performance. Without practice, there is no polishing, no understanding of the music, and therefore, no learning and no progression.

Everyone practices. But why do some pianists get better results while others do not? What makes a practice session effective?

Many students, especially the young and those in the lower grades, think that practice means playing the whole song all the way from beginning to end as many times as possible. That is not practice. That is merely playing through a piece.

Before I start to talk about how to practice, let me make it clear about why we have to practice. Some children do not understand why they are forced to practice, so they believe falsely that practice is a chore and torture meanly cast upon them by their teachers and parents. Other students think that taking less time to practice to perfect a piece means they are better at playing; thus, when they discover in disbelief that it actually takes them much longer to work on a song than they originally thought it would, they get upset and even go so far as to give up on their practice altogether.

WHY DO WE PRACTICE?

We practice in order to understand a piece of music in terms of its musical content, structure, expression, character, and style. We practice to understand the little details of the piece, the phrasing, the dynamic layout, the articulation, the movement of the melodic lines, the rhythm, and the tempo, etc.

We practice to perfect our playing of the music. After we understand the music, we still have to learn how express it with our own interpretation. We transfer what we know in our brains to our hands and through our hands at the piano. Then through the piano, our understanding and emotion about the music reaches the audience. And the platforms of such musical expression vary from lessons to performance, exams and competitions.

HOW SHOULD WE PRACTICE?

Practice is completely different from performing or an actual rendition of the whole piece in front of an audience (or even a teacher). When we practice, most of the time we do not go through the whole work (unless it is intended for beginners). We do not hear the whole song all the time completely from beginning to end. Most of the time, we merely hear bits and pieces, a phrase here and there, or we even practice one note just to find the perfect balance of weight and tone.

Practice means drilling difficult moments of a piece in progress. You can first play through it all once or twice in order to locate the problems you have with the piece. Then you mark down the areas you have trouble playing, work on each problem with concentration and patience, tackle them all one by one, and eventually put the whole piece back together for a solid inspiring performance.

Practice is like putting the small pieces of a jigsaw puzzle together. Depending on the level and the duration of that piece as well as your own level of ability, that puzzle could be 500 pieces or 10,000 pieces, and it could take you one week or one year to complete that puzzle.

The start is always the hardest. You have no clue where you should start. But after you start putting the pieces together with lots of patience, especially at the beginning, you will find more clues that lead you to the next chunk of pieces. The chunks you do put together will combine and become bigger, as you spend more effort and time on the while. You will start to see the bigger picture and get more information about what to do next. What's more, you will find that piece increasingly interesting to work on and create the best performance of it.

Practice is objective, organized, and rational.

STEPS FOR PRACTICING

Let me give you some specific guidelines on how to practice well:

1. SET A GOAL FOR EACH PRACTICE SESSION

Before you start your practice, always have a plan in mind. You cannot merely say, "I want to improve my playing" and expect the best results.

What do you want to improve on? Is it the accuracy of the notes in the right hand? The rhythm in the left hand? The fingering? Or a particular technique or movement (e.g. wrist or arm movement)? Or perhaps tempo adjustment?

When you know exactly what you want to work on every time you practice, you can accelerate your progress in polishing a piece with precision and focus in both your practice and playing.

2. PRACTICE SMALL SECTIONS OF EACH PIECE

As I mentioned earlier, do not try to play the whole piece from beginning to end a thousand times in the same way and expect that it will just naturally get better. Einstein wisely said, "Insanity is doing the same thing over and over again and expecting different results." I want you to be wise and sane about your practice too.

Sometimes you can have fun and just play a piece through, but that is not practice. When you practice, you need to have set specific and small goals to work on. In general, eight-bar phrases are commonly found in music with a regular phrase structure (more often in but not exclusively to Classical pieces only. You can mark bars 1-8 as phrase 1, and bars 9-16 etc. You can then start by practicing each phrase to find out if there is any problematic phrase that you cannot play through smoothly.

Sometimes that plan is not even specific enough. If not, you can try breaking an eight-bar phrase into two four-bar sub-phrases. For instance, you can mark bars 1-4 as phrase 1a, bars 5-8 1b, and so on (or simply mark bars 1-4 as phrase 1 and bars 5-8 as phrase 2, etc.). Try playing each four-bar sub-phrase only. Stop right at the very last note and do not go further – many students have a hard time stopping, and I do not know why. Playing more does not mean you are better, and the same goes for playing faster! Learn to control yourself. You need to stop, listen, and check to see if there is anything you still need to fix.

Another way to practice is to find a particular spot to fix, e.g., problem 1: bars 14-16 and problem 2: bars 20-22. You can also fix the same kind of problem in one go-through. For example, you might write down "notes" as one target category (bars 14-16, right hand; bars 20-22, left hand), "rhythm" as another, "fingering" and "motion" (technique) etc. Most important is that you identify what specific problem occurs in those certain bars and focus on fixing that problem alone.

In short, be more specific and creative with your practice.

3. CHECK YOUR TEMPO

I also find that many students have a problem slowing down. They believe playing at a slow tempo means their playing is not good enough, even when the music is supposed to be slow! Always work at a tempo slower than you think you can play. Play and listen at the same time. Listening to your own playing is completely different from merely hearing it. Always practice with a focused and clear mind, and you will realize where the playing is going wrong even without your teacher pointing it out for you.

If practice becomes truly mindful, it becomes more effective.

Use a metronome at times to check against your own tempo. To be honest, I do not like using a metronome much myself, but I do know it does help to check the tempo from time to time. Thus I often use it for myself and especially for my students. You still have to be able to keep a steady pulse on your own though even when you are not playing with a metronome. To that you need to ultimately establish a strong inner pulse.

You will always find that you are rushing at easier spots or faster rhythm, or slowing down at difficult phrases. To counteract that impulse, set a target tempo for your work. Play under that target tempo, and do not go faster.

Let's say your target tempo is 120. You start around 88 and practice at the same metronome marking a few times, e.g. five times, depending on how well and secure you can play at that tempo (meaning you might need more than five practices, maybe ten or even more to play with control and certainty at the same marking). Then push the marking to 96, 104, 112, and 120. I also suggest you play faster than 120, so try 128 and 132, if possible. The reason is that when you are nervous during a performance or exam, there will be a natural tendency to play a little faster than your regular tempo. Therefore, when you have practiced and played at a tempo a little faster than your regular tempo, even if you are really playing faster during a performance, you will know that you can control everything with confidence.

4. LISTEN TO THE TONE QUALITY OF YOUR PLAYING

We all know about dynamics: **f** means loud, **p** means soft, etc. That is volume.

Tone quality is an entirely different matter.

When I say "tone quality", I mean the evenness or smoothness of the sound and that of the volume among the notes of a melody. Is there any unnecessary accented note in the same melody? Does the crescendo/decrescendo really sound gradually louder/softer as you intend it to be? We always pay attention to the beginning of a melody, but how about the end? Is the ending note too loud because you do not care to place it carefully when you're hurrying to the next melody? How about the bass line? Can you hear the sound of its starting note and that sound of the phrase as it unfolds? Is the sound you are making too abrupt or too harsh?

Unless instructed to do so in the score (is found in contemporary music if so), in most cases, we want bright, shiny, round, focused, ringing sound, not edgy, ear-piercing, thin, harsh, or abrupt dead sound. Even when using soft tones like *pp* and *ppp*, we should project a clear, mellow tone, and one that is not too blurry. (The softer tone would be blurrier compared to the louder tone, as the attack of keys by the fingers is slower in speed in general.).

For pianists at a higher performance level or college-level students majoring in piano performance, for example, tone quality is a crucial element as it signifies your attainment of a higher level of performance. Unfortunately, such aspect is often ignored.

5. SING EACH VOICE IN THE PIECE

Students often have a difficult time trying to sing whenever I ask them to do so. I cannot really understand why. People in general, from children to adults, shy away from singing. Singing is the most natural way to understand how to shape a musical phrase in your piano playing. It is also nice to sing and a great way to enjoy music!

When you sing, you can easily understand where the rise and fall of a phrase occurs and which note should be emphasized and which should be delivered more lightly.

The best way to sing each voice is to sing in *solfège* or *solfeggio* (a system for singing notes, basically singing do-re-mi-fa etc.). I personally prefer the "movable-do" system over the fixed "do" system. For those who are not familiar with the two systems, "movable-do" follows the key the music is in, so if the music is in C major, then C is "do", and when the music is in G major, G is "do" (and for the minor keys: in A minor, A is "la", and D minor, D is "la" etc.). On the other hand, the "fixed-do" system is the one where C is always "do" in C major, no matter what key the music is written in.

When you sing, you should sing following the dynamic indications and the articulations.

You can also try singing one voice while playing another. For example, sing the top melodic line while playing the accompanying part with the left hand. If you can sing and play at the same time, your brain-hand coordination is pretty good, and in fact, such coordination is also very much needed in one's playing. It is also quite challenging and yet fun to do both in this way!

6. PLAY THROUGH THE WHOLE PIECE FROM BEGINNING TO END WITHOUT STOPPING ANYWHERE

After you have fixed the problems and the little details in each phrase and section, it is time to put the whole piece together. After all, the whole point of practicing is to play a piece smoothly and continuously from beginning to end and do so non-stop. Right?

Playing through the whole piece completely also allows you to see whether you have actually fixed the problems during your practice or have not. The process of practicing by phrase or section gives you an opportunity to test whether you can play through the whole piece as well. Let me give you an example:

You have divided the piece you are practicing into 12 phrases (3 sections, 4 phrases per section) as follows:

- Day 1   Fix phrases 1-2.
- Day 2   Fix phrases 3-4, put phrases 1-4 together (first section done).
- Day 3   Fix phrases 5-8 (phrase by phrase).
- Day 4   Fix phrases 5-8, put phrases 5-8 together; then put phrases 1-8 together (now you have 2 sections done).
- Day 5   Fix phrases 9-10; play through phrases 1-10.
- Day 6   Fix phrases 11-12, put phrases 9-12 together; play through phrases 5-12 together (2 sections); play through the whole song slowly

and steadily (phrases 1-2); mark down which phrase/section still has problems.

Day 7   Fix the problems marked in Day 6, then play through each section separately; then play 2 sections together (first and second sections), then play the whole song again at a steady slow tempo. Finally, play the whole song again at a moderate tempo.

By the end of Day 7, you should have finished the process of practicing the entire piece and be ready to go on to your lesson.

Whenever you play through the whole piece, treat it as a performance, even in a lesson or when you are practicing on your own. Once you get used to this idea, it will become much easier to play through a complete piece in any situation, because the state of mind when performing a piece before an audience is more or less the same. Of course you will be more nervous in a concert, an exam or a competition, but at least now you have trained yourself with the right focus and mindset.

Of course, this simple plan is only applied when learning a new shorter piece at the lower grade levels, and you would need much more time and detailed plans to practice longer and more complicated pieces. The idea of planning and scheduling your practice however is essentially the same.

Just keep working on this process every week when you are learning longer pieces. If you want to get a new longer piece ready in a week, you will need to spend more time every day on practicing it. If the piece is way too long for you to finish in a week (e.g. 8 pages), just set a realistic goal and see how much you can accomplish in one week's practice (perhaps 4 pages, or even 2 pages). Also, discuss with your teacher what target you can realistically meet for the coming lesson, as if you want to learn something in an actual lesson, especially those at higher performance levels, you need to have at least the basics done (notes, rhythm, steady slow tempo, simple dynamics and articulation). Otherwise the process will be a waste of time for you and the teacher. (Hey, you do not need your teacher to tell you the correct notes or rhythms, do you?)

    The above steps are some of the ways you can conduct your own practice. Can you think of more ways to add to these steps? Remember, practice is a very important element of piano learning. Be creative about your practice, and you will find that practice is actually a lot of fun!

THE MOTIVATION TO PRACTICE

In the previous chapter, you learned why you have to practice. Now, I want to explain how you can motivate yourself or your child to do that practice.

Let us look at some different case scenarios here.

CASE SCENARIO 1

Your Role: The Parent of a Young Piano Beginner

At the beginning, young beginners are always eager to go to their lessons. They love music, they love playing (or banging) on the piano, they love singing, etc. They tell you how much they love going to their lessons. You as a parent are pleased and believe it was the right decision to give your child some piano training.

After the "honeymoon" period, however, things change (such "honeymoon" period lasts for two to six months, depending on the patience of your child).

Your child becomes reluctant to go to the lessons: s/he refuse to practice. S/he cries before the lessons. You start to wonder what is going on here. Why did everything change? Is there something wrong with the teacher? Has your child lost interest in the lessons? Did you do something wrong?

At this point, I have to ask you a question: do your kid like studying, doing homework, or revising for upcoming tests and exams?

There is a huge difference between playing the piano and practicing the piano. And you have to talk about this issue with your child, no matter how young s/he might be.

Usually at the beginning, a teacher will be more lenient toward your child, as s/he is young and unfamiliar with private lessons. The teacher may also be more generous and praise every little thing your child does to keep up his/her interest. After a while, however, the teacher starts to expect more progress. At the same time your child is still in the mode of "having fun" and playing along. It is now time to adjust your child's mindset. It is not to say we don't have fun in lessons but we also need practice to improve and frankly, to have more fun in the long run! When this moment occurs, you should talk to the teacher and discuss what you both can do to motivate your child together. The teacher only sees the student once a week and therefore does not know your child better than you do! Keeping the communication channel open between you and the teacher helps your child grow healthily and progress happily in this new musical journey.

CASE SCENARIO 2

Your Role: The Parent of a Graded Student

Your child has been studying the piano for a couple of years and has completed some graded exams, competitions, and performance. S/he seems to forget why s/he started in the first place. With all the work at school and the activities outside school, your child starts to find reasons not to practice, like "I have too much homework to do and many tests to study!" and "But I am tired and I want some rest/fun!". What should you do?

You can first ask if your child really do have too many extra-curricular activities. Football, ballet, arts and crafts, extra tuition? The list goes on and on. Maybe there is really too much to do and too little time to rest and play, or even too little time to sleep! Of course then, anyone would reject practicing the piano. Sometimes it is not because your child does not like playing the piano, but because s/he has so much to accomplish s/he gets tired of getting all the things done after school. You might want to talk to your child and discuss whether s/he wants to continue piano or not. Try to cut down some activities too if you can. Your child's health is also very important.

Also talk with the piano teacher about your child's seemingly loss of interest in playing and lack of motivation to practice if that happens. Ask how the teacher can help. Usually there will be a few things the teacher can do if s/he are helpful and does care about your child's progress. On the other hand, you should let your child become more responsible for his/her own practice at home. You as a parent cannot take care of your child's practice all the time, as you have work to do and other tasks in life. As your child grows older in age and matures, s/he should start taking on responsibility like finishing his/her homework on time and practicing on his/her own, following the teacher's instruction.

Sometimes when you just let go a little more, you will see that your child can really do it on his/her own term. It might seem difficult to do that at times, but if you do, you will see the results gradually, maybe even right away.

CASE SCENARIO 3

Your Role: The Teenage Student

First, let us talk about you. You are the teenager. Congratulations! It's great that you are reading this book at this age! That would mean you have achieved certain levels of ability, and you are mature enough to read this (or to be forced to read this by your mom or dad!).

So, can you ask yourself why you want to practice? After all, there is no actual rule saying you have to practice every day for a certain period. Indeed, you are old enough to make a schedule on your own and decide when and what to practice and for how long.

Make a practice diary. A nice one! Write down the pieces or scales you do every day. You can also write more specifically about what you have worked on for each piece.

You can negotiate with your parents beforehand about what award you would like after you have finished the week's or the month's practice, or perhaps for a longer period of time, perhaps after a competition or an exam. But do not get greedy. Let us play the game fair and square for both parties. Okay? Whatever award or gift you are given for your playing or practice, you should understand that you are doing what you're for your own good.

I know it sounds like I am preaching to you right now. But you know what, I was a teenager once too. I know how it felt when there was a bunch of homework and revisions to do, activities after school and on the weekends, and those interesting chit-chats and hangouts with friends that were fun. Yes, I know all about that. And just like I did, you think the friends who do not play an instrument are the lucky ones, because they don't have to practice!

Let me tell you something else. What might seem fun now does not mean it's good for us in the future. When we want to be good at something, we have to work for it and at it.

Learning to play a musical instrument is just that: We work hard and try our best to be good at it; we spend time on understanding a piece and practicing on the piano with different methods. Sometimes it might take a shorter time to finish, while at other times it takes much longer than we expect. I probably shouldn't say this, but you will understand this point when you are older or more mature. You can also be really mature and try to understand it now!

CASE SCENARIO 4

Your Role: The Parent of a Teenage Student

Yes, you may not understand your child. Your child believes s/he is not a child anymore but you believe otherwise. S/he is starting to have a mind of his/her own and not want to listen to you. Oh my, that's a problem, so what should you do?

You do nothing. You just observe. You can talk to the teacher more often and discuss your child's progress. But do not nag your child. Believe me, nagging does not work. Either s/he does what you tell him/her to do just to please you or stop you from nagging, or s/he refuses to do what you ask him/her to do simply out of pure rebellion (even though sometimes s/he was planning to do the work anyway!).

Teenagers bond with their teachers easily, especially when they admire them. But if that is not the case, find out if your child does have some issues with the teacher. If there is a compatibility problem between the two parties, or if the teacher is just not really suitable for your child, it might be time to make a change.

CASE SCENARIO 5

Your Role: The Adult Student

There are plenty of tasks to do: Work, sports, entertainment, chores, laundry, dinner, or simply enjoying some time off. Everything needs time to finish it. So does piano practice. No one is there to remind you to practice anymore, because you are not a child now.

When you were younger, your parents would tell you to practice. Now, perhaps your teacher will remind you once in a while. Of course, practice is important, and you know that. Practice makes perfect (almost). But there are just so many things one can do, and hey, skipping one or two days shouldn't hurt. Or even a week's lack of practice is not a big deal. Next week you'll make it up. Or perhaps the week after next. But this month I have all these projects to do, and friends to meet up with, so I guess next month will have to be the choice. Then I'll have more time to practice. And so on and so forth. The litany is endless.

No. You do it today. Even if for just 5 minutes. 10 minutes. 15 minutes. Do it here and do it now. Do not ever view practice as a chore. Think about practice as entertainment, a pleasure like fixing something, making a meal. When you do that, you need to sort out the ingredients. That is exactly what you do in your practice. It's like putting a puzzle together, or reading a detective story, or watching a crime investigation movie. You find the leads, the suspects, the clues to the answer and solve the case. Think of practice as being easy because in fact, it is. All you have to do is focus and spend time and effort on the task.

The truth is, the more you improve through practice, the more you will want to practice, because you'll recognize the true relationship between playing and practice. You will start to enjoy your practice sessions more and more as you become a better player. Trust me. It is really that simple a choice to make and then keep at it.

The solution to the whole piano learning and practice matter is the answer to one simple question:

Why do you or your child want to play the piano?

I offer you that answer in the next chapter.

CHAPTER NINE
WHY DO YOU OR YOUR CHILD WANT TO PLAY THE PIANO?

First of all, why do we learn music in the first place?

Listening to music is one of the greatest joys in life. Making music gives us a more profound sense of enjoyment and a deeper understanding of this beautiful universal language. Providing yourself or your children with a musical education is a wonderful gift that will last a lifetime.

For decades, different studies have shown both explicitly and subtly the many benefits of music learning, including improving one's IQ and enhancing children's learning capability in all areas of learning even in more academic subjects like mathematics and languages.

Piano training is a great way to train one's mind and develop good discipline, and it requires both physical and mental coordination. To start with, it is difficult enough just to coordinate both hands together and play materials with different notes, rhythms, articulation and dynamic markings. Then we must use our feet to control the use of pedals, changing frequently without even coinciding with the hand movements at times. We also need to understand and present the various styles and forms of music by various composers in different periods and genres. And on top of that, with all the information we have learned and digested, we must listen to our own playing, create our own interpretation with control and precision and modify continuously for perfection. Indeed, piano playing requires concentration, coordination, intelligence and memorization – all are skills that are valuable to living and enjoying life.

WHEN SHOULD A CHILD START LEARNING THE PIANO?

I would say that answer is usually no younger than age 4. It is very hard for a very young child to sit still and concentrate on a 30-minute lesson every week. It is also difficult for the child to understand the teacher's direction, react to it, and perform. It takes time for a child at a young age to adapt to this new learning concept, but it is good training and it requires patience from the child, the parents, and the teacher, especially during the first six months of lessons.

The progress may seem slow and even minimal during the first year, depending on the learning mode and the maturity of each student. Do not expect a child to play something fancy very quickly at the beginning. It's usually quite the contrary, so we must take time to build a solid foundation of piano playing and musical concepts right from the start. The fancy playing will naturally come later.

If you really want your child to receive music education earlier than 4 years old, I suggest you bring him or her to a music group class offered at many music centers or childhood music education centers. In those classes, toddlers learn rudimentary music knowledge and at the same time enjoy music-making and social interaction with other children. Examples of these programs are Music Together, Kindermusik, Dalcroze Eurhythmics, and Kodály Method.

HOW DO YOU CHOOSE A TEACHER?

You must understand right at the start that it is of the utmost importance to choose the right piano teacher, especially the first teacher, for that precious you and your precious child. Although a student might have many piano teachers throughout life, the first teacher will determine how he or she feels, thinks, and responds to his or her musical training. It also depends on the kind of specific piano training you want for yourself or your child.

Before looking for a teacher, think about what you want for yourself or your child. Do you want you or your child to feel the joy of music? Or do you just want to pass exams in the shortest period of time? You should look for a suitable teacher who can fulfill these personal requirements. Don't only look at the qualifications of a teacher or even how many years the teacher has been teaching (or how old he or she is). When you find the teacher with the desired potential, just contact the person first. Have a meeting with the teacher and prepare some questions to ask him or her.

If you can schedule an interview with the teacher or set up a trial lesson, that is even better. You can get to know that specific teacher better. If not (some teachers do not offer this opportunity), then try the teacher for a month and see how you or your child react to the lessons and the teacher.

Other than professional qualifications and teaching experience (the teacher should have more qualifications than piano diplomas by exams only), you should also look for a teacher who has some performance experience and knowledge of piano teaching methods and music in general. Look for someone who is passionate about teaching, music, and the piano, compassionate toward students and children, and possesses good communication skills with both the parents and the students. The best way to find a teacher is of course through a referral or suggestions from friends and family.

WHAT HAPPENS IN A PIANO LESSON?

Piano lessons should include more than just learning a few pieces and some scales for an upcoming exam or competition.

First of all, these lessons should be pre-planned and well structured, according to a progress plan made by the teacher after further discussion with the parent and the student. In general, the teacher should teach basic piano techniques with a list of suitable exercises and pieces appropriate for the student's level and ability. The teacher should also teach the student the rudiments of general music theory and aural training. When the student has reached a certain level, the teacher should teach the student the basic keyboard harmony or improvisation techniques that are important for building musicianship.

The teacher is also responsible for teaching the student how to practice at home, applying efficient practice methods and plans. On the other hand, the parent and the student are responsible for getting the practice completed according to the teacher's instructions before each lesson.

Without practice, there is nothing that your teacher can do, even if your teacher happens to be the best piano teacher ever in the whole wide world.

FINAL THOUGHTS

I hope you understand now that music is something you or your child can enjoy and be educated in, and playing the piano is one of the best ways to achieve these two goals. You are also likely believe that you or your child has to work hard and practice in order to play the piano better, instead of trying to find the easiest and shortest route to that skill. Therefore, you understand that playing the piano is about the process, not the goal, and it is a skill intended for a lifetime. Help yourself or your child to practice in a strict and systematic, yet positive and encouraging, way. Consult and discuss the learning with your teacher from time to time and learn about the progress and problems involved in that learning.

You may want yourself or your child to take part in exams and/or competitions, yet at the same time, you understand that both are merely milestones and guidelines to achieve along the long and winding path of piano learning. Lastly, find a teacher who is well informed about piano performance and piano pedagogy and is a kind, loving and passionate personal individual who loves music, learning about it, practicing it and presenting it for enjoyment by all.

VIDEOS

The Technique Transformation Course Series and the Technique Transformation Exercise Book Series Videos referred to in the text can all be accessed free of charge on the Teresa Wong School of Music YouTube Channel.

The link is:

https://www.youtube.com/user/wwwteresawonghk

AFTERWORD

This is the first book I have ever written on piano playing, and I wanted to make it short and simple. What I wanted to do is to share my knowledge with you, so you can become better at your own playing.

I hope this book helps you in many ways, lets you realize that playing the piano is not just about moving the fingers, but rather is the harmonious motion of the whole body. The way we think and feel does affect how we play in an influential way that we rarely think about specifically. More understanding of every aspect of piano playing will give you greater strength and more confidence – physical, intellectual, spiritual and emotional – in your own playing and practice.

Be positive toward this book and your playing. Empower your trust in both. If you do, you will enjoy playing the piano immensely and immediately.

Go start playing that way now!

Teresa Wong
March 25, 2016.
Hong Kong

MY RECOMMENDED BOOK LIST

This list is organized in order of my best recommendation, with highly recommended at the top.

ON PLAYING

On Piano Playing: Motion, Sound and Expression.
Sándor, György. Schirmer Books, 1981.
Note: One of my two piano bibles of all time. **Highly recommended.**

With Your Own Two Hands: Self-discovery Through Music.
Bernstein, Seymour. Schirmer Books, 1981.
Note: One of my two piano bibles of all time. **Highly recommended.**

Freedom in Piano Technique: With an Appendix for Teaching-Diploma Candidates.
Last, Joan. Oxford University Press, 1980.
Note: Great book on technique. **Highly recommended.**

Indispensables of Piano Playing.
> Whiteside, Abby. 1955.
> *Note: It truly is an indispensable book (and a wonderful author) on the subject of piano playing.*

Essay on the True Art of Playing Keyboard Instruments.
> Bach, Carl Philipp Emanuel; 1753. William J. Mitchell. W. W. Norton & Co., 1949.
> *Note: This book needs no further explanation. Read it for historical and practical value.*

Piano Technique.
> Gieseking, Walter, & Leimar, Karl. Dover Publications, Inc. 1972.

Basic Principles in Pianoforte Playing.
> Lhvéinne, Josef. Dover Publications, Inc. 1972.

Modern Technique of the Pedal: A Piano Pedal Study.
> Schnabel, Karl Ulrich. Edizioni Curci, 1954.

The Complete Pianist: Body, Mind, Synthesis.
> Friedberg, Ruth C. Scarecrow Press, Inc., 1993.

The Musician's Soul.
> Jordan, James. GIA Publications, Inc., 1999.

Piano Playing, with Piano Questions Answered.
> Hofmann, Josef. Dover Publications, 1976.

Relaxation Studies in the Muscular Discriminations Required for Touch, Agility and Expression in Pianoforte Playing.
Matthay, Tobias. Bosworth, 1908.

The Act of Touch in All Its Diversity; an Analysis and Synthesis of Pianoforte Tone-Production.
Matthay, Tobias. Longmans, Green and Co., 1903.

A New Approach to Piano Playing Based on the Principles of F. Matthias Alexander and Raymond Thiberge.
Taylor, Harold. Kahn & Averil, 1982.

The Physiological Mechanics of Piano Technique: An Experimental Study of the Nature of Muscular Action as Used in Piano Playing, and of the Effects thereof upon the Piano Key and the Piano Tone.
Ortmann, Otto. Dutton, 1962.

The Art of Piano Playing: A Scientific Approach
Kochevitsky, George. Summy-Birchard Company, 1967.

The Science of Pianoforte Technique.
Fielden, Thomas. St. Martin's Press, 1961.

The Craft of Piano Playing: A New Approach to Piano Technique.
Fraser, Alan. Scarecrow Press, 2003.

Great Pianists on Piano Playing.
Cooke, James Francis. Dover Publications, Inc., 1999.

ON TEACHING

On Piano Teaching and Performing.
Waterman, Fanny. Faber & Faber, Limited, 1983.
Note: Short book yet full of great advice on performing, practicing and teaching.

Practical Piano Pedagogy: The Definitive Text for Piano Teachers and Pedagogy Students
Baker-Jordan, Martha. Warner Bros Publications, 2004.
Note: Highly informative book on piano teaching, a must-have for any inspiring teachers.

Well-Tempered Keyboard Teacher.
Uszler, Marienne, Gordon, Stewart, and McBride-Smith, Scott. Schirmer Books, 2000.

Developing Piano Performance: A Teaching Philosophy.
Camp, Max. Hinshaw Music, Inc., 1981.
Note: After explaining the finger technique emphasized in early keyboard treatises, Camp discusses how the musical and technical approach to piano playing and

teaching changed in the nineteenth century. At the end, she documents the continued evolution of pedagogical thought during the twentieth century.

Piano Pedagogy: A Research and INFORMATION Guide.
Comeau, Gilles. Routledge, 2009.

The Art of Effective Piano Teaching.
Ascari, Dino P. 1st Books Library, 2003.

Your Musical Child.
Turner, Jessica Baron. String Letter Publishing, 2004.

Raising an Amazing Musician: You, Your Child and Music.
ABRSM Publishing Ltd, 2009.

管教啊, 管教.
汪培珽. 愛孩子愛自己工作室, 2010.

少兒鋼琴教學與輔導.
但昭義. 世界文物出版社. 2007.

VIDEO RECORDINGS

Sound and Touch / Excellence in Music.
Berman, Boris. Excellence in Music, 1997.
Note: Excellent lecture and demonstration on the techniques of sound production on the piano and how to teach it.

Developing Musical Fingers: Lecture-Demonstration by Sam Holland.
Holland, Sam. The New School for Music Study Press, 1987.

Hereafter.
Gould, Glenn. Directed by Bruno Monsaingeon. Produced by Idéale Audience, Rhombus Media, in co-production with ARTE France and the BBC.
Note: Watching a true genius playing with so much attention to how sound is produced recorded and mixed is an eye-opening and amazing experience. It gives you a new perspective on the essence of sound as well as Gould.

ABOUT THE AUTHOR

Teresa Wing-Yin Wong received her musical training at Hong Kong Baptist University, where she graduated with first class majoring in Piano Performance (B.A. Music), along with many scholastic awards. She was also awarded with the Licentiate of the Royal Schools of Music in Piano Performance. She further studied at Indiana University Jacobs School of Music with scholarships, later awarded with a Master degree of Music in Piano Performance, with special interests in Piano Pedagogy and Choral Conducting. She is honored to have studied with great teachers such as Grace Lau Lively-Stones, Shigeo Neriki, Edward Auer, Jean-Louis Hagenauer (piano), David Chung (harpsichord), Carmen Telléz (choral conducting), and Carlos Montané (voice). Wong has participated in well-renowned music festivals, and she has performed frequently as a soloist and chamber musician in Europe, North America, and the Greater China. She was an accompanist for the Scuola Italia Program for Opera Singers in Italy and for various concert tours in the United States.

In her native city Hong Kong, Miss Wong was a freelance keyboard player for the Hong Kong Philharmonic

Orchestra, accompanist for Hong Kong Bach Choir, Opera Hong Kong Company, as well as conductor and accompanist at Hong Kong Children's Choir and Shatin District Board Children's Choir among many others. She has performed as a soloist and a collaborative musician at various local public venues and concert halls, and has also recorded solo and chamber music programs for RTHK Radio Four. Her recent performance engagement includes several concert appearances in China and France.

Being a versatile pianist, Miss Wong is also passionate about her teaching. She was an adjunct lecturer at Hong Kong Baptist University, and a teaching assistant at the Chinese University of Hong Kong when pursuing her research interest in historical musicology. Wong has also served as a jury in prestigious international piano competitions. Now she focuses on building her school Teresa Wong School of Music to teach students and train teachers in order to maintain a higher level of teaching quality and learning standard.

Other than hands-on teaching, Miss Wong is also passionate about helping students to succeed in various platforms apart from piano lessons. Miss Wong is the first person ever to develop iPhone applications to train music aural ability specifically for standardized exams presented by Associated Boards of Royal Schools of Music (ABRSM) and other music exam boards alike. Her first successful applications - Aural Training Grade 5 Lite (free version) & Aural Training Grade 5 (full version) - are now available on Apple iTunes Store for download and purchase. Her past projects include her charity organization "Teresa Wong Music Academy' which organized concerts and workshops to educate and inspire music lovers, students and teachers in the community. Her recent projects include publishing her new books - Piano Freedom, Piano Technique Transformation Exercise Book, and Music on Wings: Piano Beginner Course Book Series (Student Guides and Teacher Instruction Books).

Miss Wong is currently the director and principal of Teresa Wong School of Music, the chief executive officer of Music on Wings Publications, as well as a member of the Music Teachers National Association (MNTA).

www.ingramcontent.com/pod-product-compliance
Lightning Source LLC
Chambersburg PA
CBHW022107160426
43198CB00008B/386